I Saw Myself Alive in a Coffin

by Kait Quinn

Cover design by Carlos Urreta & Kait Quinn
Skull Photo by Luke Southern on Unsplash

ISBN: 978-1-7364839-0-9
Imprint: Kait Quinn Publishing

for those who feel more ghost than flesh.
i see you.

AUTHOR'S NOTE

Several of the poems in this book touch on depression and suicide. My intention is not to romanticize these but to share my experience with depression and suicidal ideation to help erase the stigma surrounding them. I want to normalize talking about these topics, as doing so makes it easier to seek help and heal.

Death, in general, is a topic that I also feel is unnecessarily taboo. I have found myself increasingly drawn to the topic of death as I struggle with my mental health. I have never faced or been close to death. I think that, combined with depression and suicidal ideation, has sometimes made me forget how real and permanent death is. While I do not think death is something we should be so afraid of that we sweep it under the rug, I don't think it's healthy to treat it as nonchalantly as I have. As I write in the second poem of this book, death should remind us to live.

In lieu of any near-death experience or major loss in my life, these musings on life and death are my way of accepting death as an inevitability and to remind myself that this one life is a gift. While I am still fighting myself to live my fullest life, writing these poems has been helping me shift my desire for death toward a desire to live. I hope they also help you choose to live and live to the fullest.

– Kait Quinn

CONTENTS

ODE TO DEATH

o, death!
o, mourning!
o, final respite beneath damp dirt!
your cold bones, your maggot chains,
your roses feeding blooming graves
bring a sort of twisted peace
to this gnawed, decaying brain.

o, sweet death, others would have you
blotted out from this world—how they toss you
to the sea, sweep you under
the carpet of earth—but i would have you
on a silver platter, with truffle and wine,
with moonlight bathing my skin, nectar thickening
between my peachened thighs.

for sun cannot shine without new moon nights,
storms cannot quench without droughts,
and life cannot blossom red and robust
without the looming shake of your wretched kiss.

o, death—do sing! do your seasonal turns!
bring me a life filled with golden hues,
seaside bliss, love to make my heart burst,
and i will promise you stately urn,
proud display on mantle, praise that hits
the lobe like honey, an ode
worthy of constellation.

WHEN I THINK OF DEATH

i think of the ossuary in kutná hora,
walls piled high and lined with skulls. every piece
of decor, from the wall art to the chandeliers,
made from disarticulated calcium.
i think about how my grandmother loved
all my pictures from central Europe,
except for the ones with the bones. *too morbid*, she said.
reminded her of death.
i told her, *they're meant to remind us to l i v e.*
i think of the mouse my cat killed last winter. how it
was unintentional, mother nature, but felt like murder
all the same. i think of my granddad's funeral, the waxen nose
protruding from the coffin i didn't dare
to peer in. i think about how long my dad stood there
staring at a body that once carried the soul of a man
who introduced me to *star wars*, taught me how to play solitaire.
how he was no longer granddad. just a carcass, dressed up.
i think of my body in a casket in a grave
dug six feet below earth's surface,
and i feel like suffocating. i think
of bells ringing through the cemetery and hope that burying
the living is a mistake we've fixed. but just in case,
i think of cremation. i think of clinging to salt or sprouting a garden
wild with roses and anemones. i think after death,
i'd like to become a tree.
or something with wings.
i think of all the days i wished i didn't exist
because i was never good at taking to air and knew
life does not blossom below the ground—it decays.
i think of all the days i pondered how i'd do it.
i think of all the days i put a bookmark in the thought
and tucked it under the mattress
all those nights i chose,
for now, to live.

I FELT A FUNERAL IN MY THROAT
after Emily Dickinson

I felt a funeral in my throat,
and the mourners, vacuous caged corpses,
kept gaping, gaping their mouths open
till it seemed that all sound was devoured.

And when they all proceeded
in their hushed walk, a fluttering like moth wings
kept feathering, feathering, till I felt
my mouth was cotton swelled.

And then I felt them lift gated door
and scamper across my tongue
with those same skeletal claws, again.
Then flame began to roar

as all the heavens were a wildfire.
And being made of spruce, my piano teeth
began to char. And I and silence a melding
I'd have never fathomed to transpire.

And then a crack in a chord
and I blistered like a maple, hit new silence
with every ashen key
and finished singing, then.

I AM DYING MANY DEATHS DAILY

i am dying many deaths daily,
meeting the ground one cell at a time,
one hunched millimeter of muscle,
one unravel of keratin thread.
every time you make me sigh and shudder,
i die a little, heaven flowing out of me
like a river, like paradise was rooted, all along,
inside me.
i think of the way my heart clenched and banged
its small heart body against my rib cage, splat
against lung, the day i realized
we were done. and i unearth that grave just to perish
all over again. and every time
the sun sets, i feel the stars in my liver dim,
moon in my uterus
beam a little less.
my blood blooms black dahlias that drip
ink to coat my stomach lining, and every night
i vomit little rorschachs and bits of pink meat
onto paper and guess
how i will die
some unexceptional thursday morning.

FICKLE HEART

My heart likes to play games
like Hide-and-Seek and Duck, Duck, Goose.
Some days my heart stains its guts
and wants onto my fresh-out-of-the-dryer sleeve.
Some days it is a bee in crisis,
collecting pollen, absorbing every color.
Some days I know who I am,
and who I am calls for you.
Some days it is a sinkhole,
an endless cavern that promises nothing
but a burning to ash,
then the hot slap of iron.

Don't ask me to smile—
I am an empty cemetery
filled with ghosts that knock and scratch,
unsatisfied with the lack
of flowers blooming
on their graves;
for most days, my heart is a series
of haunted chambers,
and I am trying to stop speaking to the dead,
but the pounding, the knocking—
god, the howling
—echoes like longing in my head.

DRAINAGE

life leaks / from my stormy irises /
look / how their ceruleans
contuse

FLICKER

i know what i am
and what i am not.
half-empty stomach,
quarter-cut heart,
disappearing bones—
the body never lies.
i am half a life,
blood drained, soul siphoned,
crescent moon at midnight.
i am never the whole sun,
only a shadow-edged piece of light
among a thousand.
i am not the first flicker
to beg for shade.
i am not the first moon
to bow to eclipse.
i am not the first body
to be so ravaged by fear
that i empty, empty, empty into paralysis.
but, fuck, i wish i were the last.
no one should know what it feels like
to be lifeless outside a grave.

A PAST LIFE IS EATING ME FOR DINNER

i'm locking the door to my past.
blaming it all on the greyhounds
and whiskey, sinister forces plotting
against me. but i told the pills
to do this, didn't i? wrote
my own elegy when i swayed
into strangers' beds, swallowed
that fifth cup of vodka and sprite
before i even got to the everclear-
spiked punch. my body was no
temple. it was a cold home where
apologies lodged in my throat,
and i filled the void in my ragged
stitched heart with broken glass
shards from the shot glasses
emptied before i bottomed out.
i lock the door to my past, quicken
the rising sun, and still
evening comes, black as charcoal,
with her fading stars, deathly silence,
hungry ghosts salivating
to feast on my sickly soul.
deep down inside, i am black with grief,
and they know it. and i know
it will not take lock and key
to cleanse these haunted bones.
but i cannot bring myself to throw
the vault open and invite these memories
to dine. cannot shake off November rains
that chill these porcelain ribs
into a self-inflicted cage.

RESPITE

Night draws down its shade
until the sun is completely blacked out
and the only lights are the flickerings
of dying stars in the distance.
This is where they settle in:
the ghosts, the memories,
the phrases that turned ever so slightly
in the wrong direction, things never spoken,
past regrets, future unknowns—
the kinds of things that mutate into monsters
after dark.

I could lie here, body tensed up,
for hours, counting the mistakes I made last week,
rehearsing conversations I won't have tomorrow,
trying to remember how your skin felt
against mine, how my tongue parted your lips.
I lie wide eyed and short breathed
until night drags into morning,
slipping into sleep just as the day blinks
its golden lid open, snapping me out of
my hour-long respite to remind me
that ghosts still linger in the daytime.

THIS BODY IS A COFFIN,

worn and harrowed.
every dusk, i fall asleep with ghosts
flashing moon soaked smiles and tossing tears
like falling stars.
every dawn, i wake up trembling
and haunted. if ghosts are spirits
of the dead, then i am a walking cemetery
of deceased love and buried feelings.
if to have loved is to be haunted,
how many lives have i departed?
how many bones do i possess?

MORNINGS AFTER

I wonder how many people are walking around wounded, unsatisfied,
heads tied and bobbing up toward the clouds like balloons.

How many metaphors for heartbreak, loss, hollow-body loneliness?
How many poems will I write before I get it all out of my system?

I wonder how many nights I've jarred you awake,
how many of your dreams I have claimed.

I've stopped counting how many ghosts of you have haunted mine,
how many poems I'll write before I get you completely out of my system.

GHOST GIRL

what flashes these pupils hold,
what beams of light, what reels of film,
what curve of cheek and slope of neck
and eyes shimmering like sunlit, fish-breath-
rippled wading pools
dancing under twilight.
o, to spill you out through my gaping irises,
her mouths tinged blue like dead lips
as she wastes away, stuck
watching past lives replay
on the backwards side of the lens.
o, to be a window to a soul,
something beating and warm
instead of a bone-hollow body,
vacant and haunted.
what skeletons this heart buries.
what disturbed graveyards.
what ghosts must walk
these long and lonely
crimson-calcium halls.

ANOTHER ONE GOES

skeleton daydreams surface.
i see you
sweet and so bright.

i step outside
broke and lonely.

another ghost, so bright,
goes by.

DEAD HEARTS ARE EVERYWHERE

i.

your name burns on my tongue.
there is a lie in every line i speak.

ii.

a shadow crosses her face,
happy and open just seconds
ago, and you wonder:
what lights did she see?
what door slammed against her eardrum?
what follows her into dawn
like a trail of soot?

iii.

grief tastes like the burnt caramel
of a memory. you try to swallow it,
banish it to the bowels, but it lodges
sticky in the throat.

iv.

you linger,
long after the campfire's
been kicked out with dirt,
in tired wisps of smoke.

v.

leaves lace to ash.
stars shred to snow.
dead hearts dig graves
in holy soil.

they're out there now,
waiting,
waiting for winter gales
to whisk them home.

WALKING WITH WHISKEY

i've been walking with whiskey,
blue with loss, black with grief.
my irises are a gathering sea.

i dress my tears and wear them
like pearls. and when i cannot spark
my own light to reach through

heartbreak's cracks, i stitch stars
on my skin, twinkling like a mock sky.
but underneath, i am dying

a thousand little deaths, squeezing shut
the throats of a thousand little mockingbirds
that once blossomed into poetry grenades

in my chest. i am a thousand little leaves
curling into the dirt, as if they never burned
like a thousand October suns.

DECAY

morning:

i found myself tangled in the leaves,
passing under dawn,
her rays etching shadow veins across
my pale, dewy skin.

your shadow passes through the trees,
always moving,
always just
out of reach.

and i just lie there,
    decaying.

DEATH BECOMES HER

if i were to stick to anything,
i think it'd be death.
i think maggots would make fine lace of me.
i think my bones would smooth against their teeth
like pearls. i think decay would become me.
i think i could be of more use to earth
under it than over.

one hot day in June, you'll find shade
under a heaving maple, flickering emerald,
swollen jade. on a dry winter morn,
when you are blue
and ravenous, you will find sap spilling
from her bark to your tongue.
you will sit against her trunk,
warm and drunk.
one afternoon, in early October,
you will look up at her crimson leaves
trembling like flames,
and you will think of me.

if i were to stick to anything,
i think it'd be feeding
the trees that shade,
that cradle and nourish.
being the ghost
that haunts you.

ASH GETS IN YOUR EYES

whir bone into powder—
fluffy white ash
harsh to the eye
like eclipse.

mourners milk tears.
flame beats salt, plucks

deceased out
at the roots, in case
the dead r i s e like women
with hair like sylvia's
and a taste for dust.

THE AGREEMENT

my skin jumps
toward the crunch beneath my soles
—like walking on bones.
my blood rushes
to the roots of the black-barked oak.
there is an under-
standing here.
we are in mutual agreement.
the living will haunt the cemetery.
the dead will go on living.
and the forest's gnarled tongues
will go on
drinking what breathes
beneath the soil,
inflating us walking corpses
like lungs.

IF DEATH WAS MY LOVER

if death was my lover, every night
would be a dark and strange transformation
soaked in unending cries splattered crimson. every morning
would be a rebirth—saltwater pearl on a monday,
cracked key piano on a thursday,
blackbirds blotting out October's red sun
after a full-mooned, silver night. i am always the last alive,
first to rise. and having endured the endless
night, death would grant me a day as anyone
or anything i want. and i would trade every
breakfast-in-bed, fresh-brewed-french-pressed-coffee
morning for a chance to fall every dawn
into skin other than my own. dusk comes and already
i smell the ocean water rising in my bones.
already my heartstrings are being stretched
taut and tuned. already the cold of death has blued
my lips while the featherings of resurrection
do their spine-bending work. what is having everything
you've ever wanted without this nightly suffering?

HOW TO DISAPPEAR
after Rae Armantrout

i.

you had been listening to the new phoebe bridgers album.
you didn't start at the beginning; you started with "moon song."
because of course you did—skipping daylight to dusk.

in a wisp of lilac-scented light,
you ghost this world, eyes elsewhere. i imagine you
settling like mist on a forest's mossed floor.
i imagine you a chameleon, burning with October,
foaming and tealing like ocean. i imagine
butterflies in your head and you are nearing the clouds,
filling them menacing with metaphor
until they burst—always a downpour—and now
you are marbled shades of grey.

ii.

do you like evaporation,
whiteout, untracing the map of our lives?

would you prefer any memory
you can take,
or would you rather forget?

this one glitches,
like it doesn't know if it wants to let go
or live.

like they don't mean the same thing.

WINDOWS TO A DEAD SOUL: A HAIKU

empty emeralds,
dead fish smacked against cracked ice,
g o n e—these irises

SEPTEMBER TRIOLET (THE SKY IS FALLING)

the sky is falling—
leaves drip from trees like rust.
what once was lush is aesthetically dying.
the sky is falling—
earth undresses her summer gown at winter's calling.
what once was breathing burns to dust.
the sky is falling—
leaves drip from trees like rust.

THE UNDRESSING

October warped and stirred
like futures in a crystal ball.
her limbs were queens draped in jewels,
her falling leaves a symphony,
her ballroom floors glass bottles shattered
into mosaics of crimson and amber,
lemon seeds and pomegranate. but by all
hallows' eve, black veils of tattered lace
drape over her boughs—a funeral rite
—wind hollowing to a wail.
and at the crow's calling,
she slips off her feather flame dress
to bare her November bones.
her branches beckon me into
her gnarled haunted palace, her autumn best
crumpled like used tea bags in the damp—
blacks and honeys seeping like little
chai rivers into the earth.
and in death's mists, i hear
the mourning sound of loons,
lakes cracking over with ice.
already i feel eyeless and gouged,
December's blankets of snow
seeping down to my marrow.
even the evergreens lose their lush;
even the sun dims her glow.
what i would give to wake once more
to October's morning golds.

WHITE LULL

911—what's your emergency?
this January quiet needs a belly laugh,
the snare drum of power lines crackling
in dry July heat, the throb of the sticky south's
toad croak and buzzing cicada army.

my head's too good at filling in the empty spaces
where August used to downpour like a hurricane
and September pierced the air like a fox scream
and October roared in like a house in flames.

now nature's symphonies are tire tracks
that go over the edge into nothing, and even the violent,
siren-and-gunfire sounds of the city are absorbed
in the accumulating piles of snow.
my eardrums convert the white lull into aching.

send me an ambulance,
something to puncture the silence,
swallow these cliff-diving thoughts
and make my heart
beat and leap and sing again.

911—what's your emergency?
this winter hush is killing me.

JANUARY GREYS

Of every winter month,
January is the quietest.
The lights flicker off,
the music stops playing,
snow is no longer laughter and magic
but solid and grey as the concrete
buried knee deep beneath it.

Seven-hour-old snow
crunches like a shattered rib cage
beneath my feet,
scarlet brambles sprawl like veins
—like life still flows
in something desolate
—and the trees are bare as bones,
now their meat has decayed,
seeped into the dirt
of their pungent graves.

Some mornings, I can't feel my nose
or the skin on my cheeks,
like I might be all bone, no blood
to warm the flesh, no fat
to hold the heat.
Some nights, I can't tell if I'm numb
or cold
or just dead asleep.

Some winter days,
the space between earth
and sky is a mirror
and I can no longer navigate
up from down,
north from south,
east from west—like drowning
only without a drop of water
seeping into the lungs;
just an ever thickening frost
threatening
to crack me open
and send me shattering.

AUTOPSY
after Donte Collins

when they cut me open,
my marbled skin will give with a shriek,
then drop from my corpse like a dead petal plummets
from a parched rose kept
too long past decay,
as if, all along, it was only a prop—
a dusty pink illusion poised
like a mirage. ladies, gentlemen: a fraud.

they'll find that an infestation of love songs
that burrow and poems that gnaw
have bit my heart down to lace,
have squeezed the air from my lungs
till they burst and ribs break—
shards of bone escaping:
little teeth in my flesh: stars
that puncture the l o n g
ache of night.

they'll find my heart is
a feeble thing,
baby bird of a thing,
dead leaf in snow of a thing,
a wheeze of a thing,
a whimper.
how did she make it this long, they'll wonder.

i will not splatter.
my blood will have congealed
into ink, gritty with salt.
each vein shriveled
like a slug. all those poems that never made it
up into the moonlight...

and in my tight sack of a stomach—
that restless, quivering beast
—they'll find all the words i ate,
walls of mauve velvet
scratched and worried down to threads,
like clawed consonants and howling vowels

had spent decades scraping
their way to the light.

when they cut me open, they'll find
that my body is not a home for organs
or a conduit for plasma. it is not
the salt sea i claim it to be.
it is a graveyard
where every man i ever loved
and everything i've never done
refuse to stay buried.

and when the plush, satin-lined crate
wheels in for my burial:
no need, they'll say.
this body is a casket.

a mortician would know.

LOVE DOESN'T BLOOM HERE

if i were to advertise my love,
it would start as a bud,
all morning dewed and looking to pink.
but this love unfolds into decay.
these petals are spoiled, this pollen laden
with haunting memories,
and you will never rub them completely
out of your skin.

my love is a daisy chain
running the length of an open corpse.

i love you, but don't touch me.
this luster is an illusion. this silver
a trick of moonlight. this whisper—
three words, eight letters—is a curse
disguised as a love spell. you'll never tell
the salt from the sugar. don't you see?
i'm trying to save you—love doesn't bloom here,
only rots.

this skin is the sickest white,
these eyes the coldest blue,
this tell-tale heart is a liar
laced with siren-throated tentacles
thirsting to pull you under.

MY EYES ARE FROZEN LAKES

my eyes are like frozen lakes—no,
i've used that. my eyes are like
contused skin, the kind that b l u e s
after death. and i know i've used that,
but i have yet to find a better simile for the slate
of my irises. like i have yet to find a better way
to say my skin is as blush ripe as a peach
in mid July. or that at least once a day, a pink peony
blooms between my thighs. and while i'd like to say
i am as flame alive as my hair, blood sticky like honey,
flesh sweet as strawberries freshly picked,
my body is a graveyard. my fingers, little purple
corpses. my joints are creaks in the night. the hollows
in my bones are home to decay while the chambers
of my heart are ivy-overgrown halls
thick with dust and ghosts of lovers past.
my bowels are one long guttural howl
stretching up to the roof of my mouth where it sticks
like hard candy to my molars before pulling my tongue
down into my throat. i am all choke. i am smudged mirrors
and dirty bedding, unidentifiable stain on the carpet,
lipstick on the coffee cup, stale bagel, haunted motel,
"no vacancy" sign flickering in the moonlight.
i am an untended garden, an orchard odor swollen
with unpicked plums—too full of rot i've yet to purge
to make room for spring to blossom.

SCATTER

i want to bear fruit,
build something out of dying,
but i am flying

into a million
different directions—ashes
scattered to the wind.

THINGS THAT ARE BEAUTIFUL AT DYING

mother earth.
all flame, then lace, then bare bones
in lunar worship.

daytime.
all neon pink and tangerine electric.
blue and violet as hydrangeas burst
from soil acidic.

cream roses in a vase.
petals starting to curl and brown.
like antique wallpaper.
like ancestral wedding gown.
like everything the light touches
turning to gold.

sylvia plath.
all pearl in clam, all phoenix rising,
all drama and morgue table dance.

love. the way you can feel burden unhinge
from bone.
the way you can feel the heart break.

stars.
how they take centuries to burn out.
how their whole existence is dying.

attacus atlas.
their dead wings flaking between two fingers
as if skin could turn mosaic
and take flight.

TESTING, TESTING

Last week they plucked cells from my cervix
like petals from a flower: you have precancer,
you have precancer not, you have...
The test results, written in fluent gibberish,
called my cells abnormal—cervical dysplasia, high-grade
squamous intraepithelial lesion, CIN 2-3.
I swear I feel cancer sprouting as we speak,
the wet pink pocked with it.

Maybe this is the universe's way
of giving me what I want: the hunger for life that comes
at death's lick.

Next week they'll shave off my abnormalities
with electrical currents—
wish they'd shave off my anxieties,
carve out ex-lovers'
names while they're at it
—study them under a microscope—you have cancer,
you have cancer not, you have—
while I clean up the mess
of my cervix falling out.

WHILE STANDING IN LINE FOR DEATH
after CA Conrad

While standing in line for death
—eyes panic roaming for a side chamber,
red haloed door,
a lever that knocks the earth
into reverse—
I turn to the stranger beside me:
how does your garden grow?

I'm still digging my throat
for seeds to sow.
My brumal lungs still coat
my lips in ice.
The warmth of the fireplace
does nothing
to melt these chilled, useless bones.

I swallow stars
and cough up ink.
The stain on the carpet
blooms into dead roses
and bloomed dahlias,
eclipses the last part of me
that felt clean.
Thank God for loneliness.
Torn wrapping paper
only hides what's real
for so long.

How do you crawl up
from rock bottom?
Where do you find hope
from the bowels of a tomb?
What happened to all the exits?
He must think me strange,
but in the end,
what does it matter,
being all bone and barren?

TOMB

Sometimes I feel uncomfortable in my body,
the way it can't decide between hot and cold,
the way it aches without sleep, without stretch,
with food, without food, for no reason at all.
The way anxiety hits me in the stomach
and depression settles in the lungs like rocks.
The way your tongue and hands can crack my ribs
and scramble my heart, even from a distance.
The way it is a weight too heavy for my soul to carry,
the wires in my brain unfit for wings.
The way it is a cage, a prison sentence, a tomb.
And I know the ways in which it is also a miracle,
why we say, *worship it like a temple.*
But some days I understand the longing for death
in the simplest way—the wish to unzip, unhinge,
crawl out of skin and fly, soul bare,
into freedom.

ALL MY WORST

i've been sickening at the core.
been tossing myself against my bones
hoping to puncture
skin and crack out of myself,
like this body is a shell and i have yet
to really be born.
i've been breathing dreams like air,
sipping all the gore that splatters my skull
the nights i take hydroxyzine,
ex-lovers via mouth when i don't.

last night i dreamt i lost my home,
dreamt everyone admonished me
for doing everything wrong,
swore i was losing you to a woman
who could give you more, and i spoke out loud
the words i've never spoken to anyone.
i woke up feeling utterly useless.
i woke up choking on salt,
longing for an ocean to drown in.
i woke up wanting
to vacate this body, this timeline
for one in which
i could start over as anyone
but me.

SOUL STRETCHED

soul stretched to its confined limits / my skin weeps / salted crimson

I AM I AM I AM

i am kait quinn.
the year is 2020.
i am in Minneapolis.
the cat is seven.
i am thirty-two.

most of the time i am,
but right now i am miles away.
i am seventeen and drowning
in icy pools of irises
as blue and grey as mine.
i am nine and cracking elbow
clean in half. i still feel it sometimes.
still believe the joint has bent
completely back.

i am kait quinn.
the year is 2020.
i am in Minneapolis.
the cat is seven.
i am thirty-two.

most days i am, but today
i am in a fever in Texas.
i am seeing stars and can't stop
looking at us in mirrors,
searching for an alternate universe
where you're still kind to me
and everything is reversed.
i am sixteen with bruised lips
and a heart gone cold
before she even bloomed.

i am kait quinn.
the year is 2020.
i am in Minneapolis.
the cat is seven.
i am thirty-two.

most of the year i am,
but this year, i am twenty-two

and falling in love and everything is still
butterfly dizzy and clothes
unpeeling quick, quick, quick
from soaked skin.
i am twenty-one and wasted,
being groped by a stranger
in the pitch-tar dark.
i am doll still.
i am screaming inside my head—
movemovemove—and i lie still
as a statuette.

i am kait quinn.
the year is 2020.
i am in Minneapolis.
the cat is seven.
i am thirty-two.

most moments i am, but here,
now, i am eighteen and dizzy drunk
on smiling, fit so snug
in my first and only found family,
and i'll never admit it in my poetry,
but o, i am happy. i am happy. i am
fifteen and draped
in oversized blacks, scribbling furiously
in my journal and no one notices me.
no one wants me.
no one knows.
i become less flesh and more ghost.

i am kait quinn.
the year is 2020.
i am in Minneapolis.
the cat is seven.
i am thirty-two.

most of the time i am,
but today
i am invisible.

IDEATION

when nana died, i didn't blink.
stayed still. hadn't learned that emotion yet.
even when my granddad passed
in my early twenties, i didn't cry at his funeral.
didn't understand why sister sobbed
like a child, clinging to dad a l l the way down
the church aisle. a procession of mourning.
grief on display. my eyes dry as the cracked earth
that once wrapped muddy arms around a lake.
death was an intangible thing.
still is.
think that's why i call my irises contused
instead of blue.
think that's why i dream of freak accidents.
think that's why i see drips and tubes,
old lovers rushing to my hospital bed.
think that's why i sometimes hope for positives
and bad-news diagnoses.
think that's why i rabbit hole true crime,
grab plath poems with my teeth.
think that's why my mind spends weeks in bed
caressing suicidal ideation,
stroking her pallid legs, rolling her bright thumb
across my tongue
like a fat red cherry.
think a dance with death
would shake some life into me.

SURVIVOR'S GUILT

august ends
and i've come no closer to the sun.
so i go into winter
with nothing in my veins
to sustain me,
to keep my skin peached
and from shrinking to the bone.

i feel death's hover
'round every corner.
feel it like eyes with teeth.
feel every ghost—from their stones
between the weeds—
resenting me in silence.
waiting
for lightning to strike,
my cracked heart to finally
give out, my bones
to join them in the grave—
earth one great globular
mausoleum we living
thoughtlessly desecrate.

why should i get to live?
why should i get to share
the earth with salt waves
i never let enfold me?
with fields of wildflowers i never
let my toes meet?
with all those lips
i let pass by
blossoming and untouched?
with so much sky
i rarely scrape?
so much soil
yet to catch
in the grooves of my soles?
so many miles of air just waiting
for warm bodies to press
a cold face against
on their way down?

i don't think enough about the bullet
that just missed me.
about the gallons of the pacific
that could have drowned me,
had i not found my way to the surface.
all those stacked skulls
in that little Austrian ossuary.
why the undertakers dug them up,
painted and piled them there.

i spend so much time afraid.
so much time stagnant.
so much time waiting
for death to breathe at my door
and shock me into living.
and every day death does not come,
i swallow another pound of guilt,
rooted legs sinking ever deeper
into this cemetery we call an earth.

DEATH-AGONIES

the moon has died,
been spirited away,
ripped from sky
like mole from flesh,
like bones from grave,
like wildflower from roots—
an umbilical snap
it cannot endure.

summer's in decay.
spring's only a memory.
already i can feel all futures
withering to dust.

i grow tired of all
these death-agonies,
and yet i cannot stop
filling mason jars
with bouquets of cut peonies.
they'll decay whether i snip them,
rip them from root or whether they stay
unplucked. but at least here,
on my writing desk,
they can be admired,
not hidden behind some shed,
veiled by the maple now reaching
out of the yard and into the street
in all her yellow look-at-me glory.

what a cumbersome weight
we carry: trading death for these
temporary satisfactions.

SUSURROUS NIGHTS

the fox hears the rabbit screaming.
it is a terrible thing, twist of a knife,
portrait of a throat on fire.

what is it like to be god?
to be cinder blooded?
to weave dreams into nightmares?
be the thing that goes bump in the night?

it is hysteria.
it is black roses
and ash-burnt lungs.
it is beating the wind
with raven wings,
stirring skies into phantoms
and moonlight into tricks.
it is crumpled paper in a fire,
disintegrating,
as if it never was.

these susurrous nights, eden sinks
into grief, wails and whips
autumn into melodies that wrap
like ivy
within the crystalline cracks
of my broken soul.

the night twists me
full of ghosts.

the rabbit screams,
and i shatter.

IN THE BREAKDOWN

there was no peace for me in the neatness
of tied bows and scarlet roses,
dew fresh and tidy
in their full perfect blooms.

i only ever found comfort
in the trees' crimson fading,
the death of things, the cracking open,
ash smoke thick and spilling.

i only found solace in the breaking.

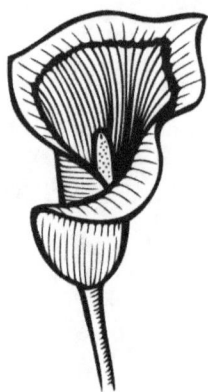

I SAW MYSELF ALIVE IN A COFFIN

i saw myself alive in a coffin.
i saw my pink skin polished porcelain.
i saw a vase
emptied of June's peonies and murky waters.
i saw a shadow like a blackbird
cross over my waxen cheeks.
and the calla lilies weep.
and the calla lilies weep.
and i want to burn this imposter
to ash. i want to resurrect.
i want to rise winged and honey dipped.
i want the chance to rebirth
a mockingbird, a maple tree,
a sunflower, a salt-veined, siren-lunged sea.
nothing will bloom from caged
and flooded roots.
only stink,
only decay,
only sempiternal death.
and the calla lilies wept.

SEVEN SHADES OF SADNESS

i. *chartreuse*

like the shift between seasons. straddling
a beginning and an ending. feeling that normally
ignored pace of time quicken across your skin.

like leaves in August. like a pot of honey,
after decades, going bad. your only options:
guzzle it down to a stomachache or let it rot.

ii. *yellow*

sometimes nostalgia sweeps in
warm, gold, and glittering.
she wraps around me like a sweater
in autumn. i feel her most
in October and remember fondly
sharpened pencils, blooming romance,
chocolate peanut butter cups melting
in my palm.

and sometimes nostalgia is sepia,
corners fading, edges frayed.
suddenly i'm all too aware of time,
and i want to go back, back, back...

iii. *blue*

it can be small as a dew drop.
still as a lake.
persistent as drizzle.
raging as hurricane.

but it's all water
carving canyons
for new blooms to fill.

it is a blessing
to f e e l.

iv. *black*

grief tugs at your heart,
the skin beneath your eyes.

sorrow
floods the corridors of your legs and arms
and all you can do is stare
up at the ceiling,
waiting for respite of sleep
to come.

v. *white*

arsenic white. hot-tin white. hospital-wall-
sterile-and-blinding white.
is-this-it white. will-it-get-better white.
giving-up white.

vi. *grey*

static numbs the air.
pins and needles building barriers
between sole and grass,
skin and skin,
honey and tongue.

there is danger here.
there is a bleeding out.

but of course,
you never know it,
unless failure shocks you
back to life.

vii. *purple*

heartbreak blossoms like
an invisible bruise—ev-
rything grows tender.

CREATION

lying lavender in the coffin
before the bloom,
flesh fraying into feathers,
home-grown constellations
bursting bright into existence
in my womb,
pupils mapping memories
i'll never visit again,

my heart is a boomerang,
skin on fire, burning
to keep me alive.
the darkness came,
and i scared it away.
death came knocking,
and i took crimson flight,
leaving behind
these drunk and dreary days.

look:
how life still flaps
in butterfly wings bitten
to November lace.

LIE NEAR DEATH

trap the spider.
silence the nightingale.
gut the flowers.
listen to the injured rabbit's wail.
count how many mornings the ambulance
pulls up to the neighbor's house,
her irish tounge warbled, her legs slower,
her yard a garden blooming in marigolds.
walk the cemetery.
look to the sloughed leaves.
lie near death and catch
the fever called living.

GO ON

i felt a searing
throw open
the doors—
you are not dead

—this fantasy of mine
rising to a crest.

i unfold my corpse,
fill void
with nectarine,
go on, go on, go on.

THE GARDEN

I dare to stride about the garden with my wrist outstretched,
its white scars gleaming in the sunlight.
My lungs take in fresh air, exhale old breath
that has rot in my chest like dead weight
for three years, going on a century, too long.

Perhaps it's spring on my tongue or the flick of silver
bouncing off my newborn flesh
that brings the chickadee to land on my palm,
like I was made of bark, and build a nest for new life
in the crook of my arm.

And I am rounding corners blindly
like I've been here before or trust my instincts
without second thoughts. And everything is so foreign,
I must be in a dream; for when my eyes are open,
only blackbirds cross my path.

MIDNIGHT EPIPHANY

autumn rains pang against my midnight window
as i slink out of bed and creak, tip-toed, over
the old wood floor, when what should catch my throat
and chill my bones but a phosphene pool
blooming in my closet, in the softest silver, as if the moon her-
self had took her try at gravity, plunged hot
through atmosphere, and of all places, landed here
in my dirty clothes basket. i do not know whether to be scared
or curious or invigorated or all of the above—for what is living
if we are not moving, with enthusiasm, toward all the fireflies
and lanterns that catch our eyes in the thick
of October fog, even when our skin puckers and bones tremble
with every forward step? and if it is a flame's flicker,
i hope it is a lamppost guarded by a friendly faun.
and if it is a pale moon witch, i hope she pulls me like an ocean
in the direction i need to be going. hope she blesses me
lustrous with a dusty kiss. and if it is the reaper, i hope
it is just a warning; for if he were to ask: *are you ready?*
i am not. i admit, there, in the hollow between
my closet doors, to absolutely no one but myself:
i've been so scared rooted, i've forgotten to live.

BETTER TO BURN

sometimes it feels like my lungs aren't moving.
sometimes i press my fingers into my neck and feel nothing.
sometimes it's as if my limbs are wrapped tight in string
until there's nowhere for the blood to go but stagnant.
so sometimes i need your hands to feel
what my dead nerves can't.
sometimes i need your eyes to catch the rose
in a mazarine sunset, crystalline seaside, burning leaves in October
because sometimes my pupils forget to see color.
and sometimes my eardrums feel busted
and i need your heart's bass to remind me
what music feels like.
and sometimes my taste buds go sour and i need your tongue
to tell me what it tastes like
to lick something ripe and sweet.
and maybe between your fingernails, your teeth,
your mechanical and electronic tinkerings,
you can find a way to unravel the numb from my senses.
grab my wrist, my waist, my hands;
make me cry, laugh, scream, feel again.
i want to b u r n life back
into this ghost-numb skin.

HOW TO UNDEAD

how to turn
dead fish to sea glass,
sad farewells
to volcanic hymns,
rotted bone
to cinnamon sticks.
shall we ask the poet
or the resurrectionist:
how do you make
a broken-winged bird
flap & trill & fly again?

INSERT HERE

insert here something
hopeful like horizon, peach
like August sunset.

something poetic
about starlight, moondust, lakes,
and silver lining.

anything to keep
heart beating, blood humming, brain
from numbing. child—b r e a t h e.

NO WRONG EVER OCCASIONED FROM FEELING THE STORM

hold up hurt to the light.
wonder weary
s m o o t h
and gold.

salt sad.
wreck heart
into a splatter—
violet and crimson
constellations blooming
across lungs.

no wrong ever occasioned
from bearing the ache,
suffering the storm;

only from the festering
of a wound
simply bandaided
and forgotten.

death will come.
her harp strings will snap.
her black bells
will toll.

be ready
for the funeral.

MIDNIGHT AT THE GRAVEYARD

moonlight swirls in fog;
wind whispers secrets
mostly ghostly while the bare
branches clink together
like bones. the ground i walk
is soft earth and plush lawn,
but i know what lurks beneath,
all pink and worming,
all stench and decay.
my skeleton can't help
but rattle. pulse can't slow
its rhythm. and i imagine gobs
of my own damp, contused skin
melting off my limbs,
eye sockets crawling
with maggots, their teethy little
mouths guzzling my flesh
down to the bone. we fear this
wasting away. say natural's not in it,
burn or embalm.
i think of what it means
to not exist. i think about how everything
wild becomes a meal,
then a carcass, then back
to the stardust and earth
that birthed it. i think
it is not death
but the unknown that we fear—
all those fairy tales we concoct
to put our minds at ease.
all those centuries of falls
and we have yet to learn
from the leaves.

EDEN SINKS INTO GRIEF

the fox hears the rabbit screaming—
we brush it off as phantom wind.
the elk sees shadows slip
between moonbeams—we call it
a trick of the light.
the wolf tastes the deer's death,
wears it on her jaw like lace—we believe
the poor thing will rise
whole and unbleeding
in some paradisiacal eden.
we do not have to do everything,
we just have to be
(relatively) good; our second life
(eternal) awaits. meanwhile,
earth gnaws the doe's carcass
down to bone, then ash; then, it's as if
she never existed. death knocks on our door
daily, yet we go on
passively living in our hollow coffins,
believing time stretches like a road
circling and circling the globe. but no such
road exists. every patch of land meets ocean.
everything has an edge.
how will you meet yours?

OUR HELL
after Emily Haines

our hell is not rooms
stifling with iron, disease.
our hell is ripe words

buried in tongue's tip,
untold stories, unturned leaves;
where ghosts go to cry.

CALL IT A BLESSING

lana croons in the moonlight
that happiness is a butterfly—
something that can't be caught,
only held for a moment.
so what does it mean when six little legs land
on your open palm,
stay,
wings spread like a crescent moon?

i call it a blessing. i call it an omen.
i call it a reminder that all things are fleeting.
i am reminded
that earth turns through seasons.
that at every moment she is ripe
for a meteor strike.
that one day a butterfly will probe my skin
for its last golden drop of honey,
wings catching sunlight
like stained glass.
that i will slip into the dark and scatter,
on the softest wind, like ash.

i will scrape my tongue of apologies.
untuck the songbird from my throat.
toe the edge without fear.
eat the cake without guilt.
lick the icing off your lips
while i still can.
i will train my pupil on every slippery sunset
like it's my first, worship every moonrise
like my last. remember
that we were happy here.
welcome the storm
like an offering.

FALL

it's autumn leaves.
it's shooting stars.
it's bird's first flight.
it's not complicated.
that is the beauty of falling.

float down into these pleasing
aches, these butterfly wings
fluttering rib cage like eyelashes
sweeping blushed cheeks.

this life will pass us by,
these bodies will fade to dust,
their graves will blossom
in chrysanthemums.
but today you're here
with me. tomorrow
you could be lifetimes away.

so fall
here with me now.
let's carve our love into the earth
and live forever embellished
in amber, the old trees telling
our twisting tales
for lovers and ages to come.

THE POETRY OF EARTH IS NEVER DEAD
after John Keats

the poetry of earth is never dead.
on the hottest days, when the birds have quieted
into the shade and we have retreated to our air-
conditioned caves, the cicadas continue humming
like a choir spreading humid
through a Georgia church on a Sunday.
even the thinnest thread of air
can send the wind chimes singing.
and when there are no leaves left
to whisper secrets through the woods
and winter hushes the streets in white,
there is still the squeak of a mouse caught
in the cat's jaw at midnight; still a gust of wind
pummeling snow from the branches
against the windows with a muffled thud.
the creek never fully freezes over,
still babbles on as ever o'er the rocks
by late December.
even stilled lakes creak in the night like ghosts
tip toeing across the floorboards
in perfect poetry.
even on nights too cold for crickets to wreck
the silence, you might hear a scuttle like little pink feet
scampering up into the dryer vent.
and on the coldest nights, there always seems
a howl grieving in the pallid distance
o'er our unsounded graves

WHEN I DIE

do not bury my body in the earth
to slowly rot & decay in a cage—
i have already spent
an entire lifetime entombed.
do not think of me as a corpse
but as a flicker in the distance,
a fluttering of piano keys,
a subtle shift between seasons

—i do not want to be remembered
the way i lived: sack of bones,
ankles cast in cement.
i want to ride the wind.

so burn me to ash
on a blue day in October,
dance to Beirut in my firelight,
then set me free
with the gold
& pomegranate leaves
of summers past & those yet to be.

LIVING IN SIN

express explicitly;
risk the nighttime,
the streets, and troubled seas.
forget the floral arrangements
—i'm too young to stay in.

broken mirrors. their superstitions. the fantasy of limbs laced in pearled chiffon. the ghosts that make gravestones of my rib bones. ideas of four right chords and stars in alignment. the wish that my hips will narrow and my spine will straighten. summer. disdain for winter. dull, dark, and soundless days. fear of death. all the books i've only ever let collect dust. taste for cigarettes. taste for decay. taste of your mouth on mine. the almosts of last year. the flimsy idea that you could have ever been the one. hope—to be traded for: what i want, i take. jeans that don't fit. hearts that don't stick. memories i don't know what to do with but pine over. the notion that there'll always be time—there won't. there won't.

DESTINY

our lives are novels lightly read
and bound at ever-thinning spines.
we burn as easily as paper,
like we're just waiting to be ash.
look up: this silhouette of stars
is nothing but dust,
and from birth, we are always decaying,
shedding off bits of our skin
every moment and floating back
up whence we came.
from one minute to the next,
we are never the same.

what will we burst into
in the next life?
where will our dust settle?
what pages will you fold of me now
into the crooks of your bones,
the nooks between your teeth
so that you'll remember?
what will i carry of you
into the after?
and will we?—remember?
are we destined always to meet?

WHEN WE GET THERE

we'll get there:
erect and head high or crawling on our bellies,
blood dripping over the carpet and piles of ash.
the heart pulses until it doesn't,
the blood runs hot until it's not,
the lungs are fresh baked bread
until they're snowflakes
—quiet, cold, fragile under heat of breath.

when this laughing heart faces death,
the gods will offer me the stars' canvas as ink,
saturn's rings as oil pastels, jupiter's storm
as wet acrylic. they will offer me sanctuary
in a honey-lined womb, feed me plasma and moon-
beam, smear me crimson—an unbirthing.
what will i emerge as when i crawl
pink and slick from cracked cocoon?

i hope i rise a lunar thing.
i hope i rise a pelagic thing.
i hope i rise a feathered thing,
pupils always searching
for starlight or sunbeam.
i hope i rise with with salt on my skin and fins
between my toes. i hope i rise
as ariana grande in "god is a woman." i hope
i am the kind of storm that sinks men,
coaxes curves into the sun,
nourishes ravaged ovaries
to peony flower
and pink cherry blossom.

what all must die
in order to bloom?

RESURRECTION

red and russet leaves
litter earth
like shattered glass.
drip of gold here,
drop of blood there:
break and repair,
break and repair,
like my heart leaving trails for ghosts.
stop this bleeding;
cure this aching;
come find me,
star bright and bewitched,
on the other side
of this decay.
a crow calls in the distance.
a change of scenery
unravels from horizon.
a gust of wind,
a shift of sky,
a slant of holy afternoon light
unwinds the dying
and sets October on fire.

COMMANDMENT

i will not make myself small.
i will not stand on the edge of a cliff,
try on ghost skin, pray for the courage to jump.
i will not call it quits before this body is done.
will not wipe away the blood, but i will not hide
any proof that i have bled.
i will not make myself forget the scars
bad men left on my heart, between my legs.
i will not let them bury my mauves or blacken my blues.
i will water these old wounds with salt,
patch them with amber to catch the light.
i   will   bloom
and multiply
till i stretch to a meadow where the living
can crawl from their coffins and rest
their dizzy heads;
find peace in the lavender,
hope in the anemones,
resilience in the sunflowers,
like pollen for the bees.

THE FUNERAL

I know not much of death
except that it's where we are all going
and it calls for black
and there's nothing real about embalmed bodies.
I want to be burned
before they get a chance to color me into a lie,
suffocate me in the dirt.
I am not for you in life,
and I will not be for you in death.
Don't rush into my funeral in a steam of hot tears.
Roll in on a bead of laughter
with blood pulsing through your heart and poetry oozing
from your lips; waltz
to the rhythm of my overcast-with-sun-peaking-out-
every-so-often autumn playlist; toss leaves into the air,
even if October still waits below horizon.

I know not much of death
except that I've yearned for it, made love to it,
romanticized it into a sweet release,
a warm embrace, a stroke of my hair, a whispered
there, there, enough now. But I've learned
that sun is warmer and honey is sweeter,
and there are so many sunrises left to see,
so many cobbled stone streets, so many coastlines,
so many salty oceans to dip my toes in,
so much skin to press against mine,
and so many butterflies
waiting in the crevices of my heart
to strip their cocoons, flap the wet from their wings, and fly.

The leaves may lie dead on the lawn,
but it is not my November.
So when I pass over into winter,
imprint me on your tongue, don your funeral blacks,
find somewhere sun kissed and autumnal
to spread my ashes,
but don't you dare cry—
I did not fight for my life
to be burdened in death with your sadness;
I chose to fucking L I V E.

MORTALITY

eyes take in decay,
hands
pull it apart,
throw it away.

too cumbersome,
heavy—death.

tear through fear;
fall into life.

ENDINGS ARE BEGINNINGS

the clouds are wisping like smoke.
afternoon rays slant, ever so slightly,
in the opposite direction.
trees talk riot of leaves and shattered
stained glass, while crows
cackle jokes the sun won't get.
step aside, croons mother moon.
it's my season to choose
whether to light up the night sky or milk it
for all the ink it can drip.
and being on my knees in lunar worship,
i trust that she knows
the dark has its reasons.

September ends and everything
is thrown off course.
September ends and the only dead girl
i've ever known would have turned thirty-
one or -two—we weren't *that* close,
just close enough to dream of marrying
our teenage poetry, seal it with a spine.
i still wish i would have let her take me
under her wing. wish i would have let her talk me
out of my biggest mistake, and i don't deserve
this ache, this twinge i get every last
day of September, like we ever shared more
than a lover, couple phone calls, a few poems,
handful of text messages lost to the ether.
but we could have been coffee and ink stain.
could have been vinyl and wine.

the first cold breeze of the season
fills me with both decay and a lung full
of crisp air, and sometimes dying feels like living
and i'm still trying to figure out how that can be.
i'm still reading *perks* every October.
still soundtracking autumn with "you told a lie"
and "dead end girl." still foraging fallow fields
for heartbeats swollen for the harvest.

when this is all over—when the trees have burned down
and the earth is all salt and ash and the sea
has swallowed all the stars that once smoldered
for centuries above our glowing pupils—i hope i have planted
all my wishes. hope i have sown all my shoulds,
buried all my ghosts, and sloughed
all the dead from my bones.
hope all my regrets blossom
into something with a pulse.

WHAT'S SACRED ABOUT THE MUNDANE

Sunlight slinks through kitchen window,
bringing my attention to the dust motes,
an old coffee-drip stain the size of a quarter
on the floor, and I think of all the lives
that once lived and still linger here.

Sausage sizzles like egg yolk
on desert concrete in summer,
and I forget, for a moment,
how the Minnesota earth outside these walls
is already piling with snow.

Steam dances off the dark hot spring
inside my coffee cup and reminds me of the steam
hovering over dawn's lakes and that by December,
we can say we've walked on water.

The marmalade spreads itself
across the charred toast, seeps into
burn marks, and I imagine the curls
of orange peel as pumice, amber jelly as salve
for my own dead skin and old scars
that will go on basking in someone else's sun,
and I can only hope that they
will hold me just as sacred.

AFTER DEATH

I don't know what happens after death.
But I know that after the heart stops
and the blood stills its flow
and the body stiffens to its final resting position,
there is sunrise and sunset,
glows on the horizon that paint the sky
neon, pastel, watercolor electric.
There are so many stars to wish on—
so many, that you'll never hit every one.
There are so many moon phases,
waxes and wanes, turns of life like seasons.
There are so many lips to kiss and tongues to taste
and limbs to envelop mine.
There is so much longing and ecstasy, give and take,
aching between the thighs and breaking inside the heart.
There is so much dark to swallow and light,
so much light, to spill back onto canvas,
onto paper, onto piano key and guitar string.
There is music. God, there is so much music,
and I'll never get to all of it, but I will carry every tune
I've ever fallen in love with
inside these bones until they are ash.
There are so many poems to read,
so many words to graffiti to skull.
There are so many golden summers to watch unfold
into flame into smoke into bare bone white,
then so many springs to witness the miracle
of dead things rising back to life.
There are so many words to write, so many oceans in which
to choke on salt, so many mountains to at least attempt
to climb, so many cobblestoned streets, so many ruins,
so many forest floors upon which
to deliver my wild out from womb.
There are so many storms to brew,
so much lightning waiting to strike.
There is   so   much   life
in this geranium heart yet.

DESPITE EVERYTHING

open your mouth.
let your lungs fight.
let go of the ash that awaits
beyond the miles of dark
beneath you and reach
for sun, for moon, for the candlelight
someone, somewhere set glowing
for you—i promise they have.
open eyelid. pulse pupil.
crack fist through wood and c l a w.
unhook the maggots.
divorce the flies. push
through dirt like pink-wet babe
through crimson canal.
daylight, meet skin.
oxygen, meet lung.
body, meet blood that broils
blue skin to a peach.
men broke you.
unbalanced pools of chemicals
tipped you off kilter.
life drowned you at the roots.
earth dulled your shine.
remember who you are:
child of the stars,
daughter of sun,
slivered rib of moon—your bones
are capable of glowing.
reach in, reach in, reach in.
break the dam holding in
all that water
weight, those river stones,
the pain you carry in your gut.
rush of blood.
rush of faith.
rush of light as bright
as stars and bone forming
at their cosmic birth.
remember what you are made of—
l i v e
despite everything.

NOTES

"I Felt a Funeral In My Throat" is after Emily Dickinson's "I felt a Funeral, in my Brain, (340)."

"Another One Goes" is an erasure poem of the song "Another One Goes By" by The Walkmen.

The title "Dead Hearts Are Everywhere" is a line from the song "Dead Hearts" by Stars.

"Ash Gets in Your Eyes" is an erasure poem of pages 23-24 of *Smoke Gets in Your Eyes* by Caitlin Doughty.

"How to Disappear" is after Rae Armantrout's poem by the same name.

"Autopsy" is after Donte Collins' poetry collection *Autopsy*.

"Things That Are Beautiful at Dying" was inspired by Sei Shōnagon's list poems.

"While Standing in Line for Death" is after CA Conrad's book titled *While Standing in Line for Death*.

"I Am I Am I Am" was inspired by *The Haunting of Bly Manor*, episode five, titled "The Altar of the Dead."

"Go On" is an erasure poem of pages 54-55 of *Smoke Gets in Your Eyes* by Caitlin Doughty.

"Our Hell" is after Emily Haines' song by the same name.

"The Poetry of Earth is Never Dead" is after the first line of John Keats' poem "On the Grasshopper and Cricket."

"Living in Sin" is an erasure poem of the song "Archie, Marry Me" by Alvvays.

"Mortality" is an erasure poem of the song "Body" by Mother Mother.

ACKNOWLEDGMENTS

To A.B.Baird Publications for first publishing the poems "January Greys" and "In the Breakdown" in the anthology *Solace: Poetry of Nature* (2020).

To the Instagram poetry community for being so welcoming and encouraging and for creating a safe space to be vulnerable in my poetry. Thank you for being vulnerable with me. Thank you for breaking the stigma surrounding mental health and suicide by sharing your own experiences through poetry. I could have never published this book without the acceptance, understanding, and love I've gotten from this community.

Thank you especially to the following poets whose prompts inspired many of the pieces in this collection: A.B.Baird Publishing, Afra Khan; Aggy (@chaosinline); A.J. Butler; Alexis (@_lexmwrites); Alexis M. Romo; Alley Franke; Amanda (@lemondaisypoetry); Amelie (@celestialtruce); Amy Jack; Amy Kay; Angela Lowes; Anne Sparrow; @apoemshewrote; Ariel K. Moniz; Bea Lauren Reid; Caitlin Anne; Cerys NG; Deanna M. Ramirez; David Barron; Devika Mathur; Elle (@5cand1e__lie5); Emma-Jane Barlow; @epeolatry.edits; the Eunoia Prompts team; Eve Poetry; the Falls Poetry team - @aseawords, Ashley Jane, Kelli (@attemptingzen); Gregory D. Welch; Helena (@hlnpnts); Iz (@poemsfordusk); Jasmine Higgins; Karan Chambers; Kathryn (@hailspoetry); Kristiana Reed; Laura (@laurabeingawriter); L.R. Sterling; L.T. Pelle; M. Blake; @m_is-_for_marigold; Megan (@apatheticroommate); Mei Yan; @midnight_thoughts_with_latte; the @myth.and.lore team; Natasha (@natashawritespoetry); Neya Krishnan; Nyx Blue; OlwenDaisy; @otterwrites; Paul Idiaghe; the Poets Anonymous team; @quireandquartz; Raquel Franco; Reyes (@faithisawriter); Sabina (@finding.finesse); Sam Nimmo; Sanah Singh; Serena Morrigan; Shelby (@zombearwrites); @_soulpoems; Swati Sudhakar; @thewriterchokri; and Tyler Walter.

And, of course, to Carlos for helping me take this book from a Google Doc to a paperback. I'd be lost without you. Literally. I love you!

ABOUT THE AUTHOR

Kait Quinn is a legal admin by day and a prolific poet by night. She is the author of the poetry collections *I Saw Myself Alive in a Coffin* (2020) and *A Time for Winter* (2019) and is one of eight poets featured in the anthology *Solace: Poetry of Nature* from A.B.Baird Publishing. Her poetry has also appeared in *Chestnut Review, VERSES, New Literati,* and *Sorin Oak Review.* Kait lives in Minneapolis with her partner and their regal cat Spart.

To learn more about Kait and her writing, visit her website at kaitquinn.com and follow her on Instagram at @kaitquinnpoetry.

www.ingramcontent.com/pod-product-compliance
Lightning Source LLC
LaVergne TN
LVHW051425080426
835508LV00022B/3244